100% UNOFFICIAL JEDWARD
A BANTAM BOOK 978 0 857 51122 5

First published in Great Britain by Bantam,
an imprint of Random House Children's Books
A Random House Group Company.

This edition published 2012

1 3 5 7 9 10 8 6 4 2

Text copyright © Bantam Books, 2012

With special thanks to Jaine Keskeys, and Dan Newman at Perfect Bound Ltd.

Photo Credits: Action Press/Rex Features 7 (& 40br), 30bl. Adam J. Sablich/Shutterstock.com 28tr. Adrin
Shamsudin/Shutterstock.com 21b-3. Alex Staroseltsev/Shutterstock.com 56tr. Amy Nichole Harris/Shutterstock.
com 52tr. AridOcean/Shutterstock.com 13tr. Asaf Eliason/Shutterstock.com 43br. Beretta/Sims/Rex Features
41tr, 48tr, 49br, 53l, 52bl. BlueOrange Studio/Shutterstock.com 53bl (& 59tl). Brian Rasic/Rex Features
9, 18r, 21m. Cinemafestival/Shutterstock.com 16b-3, 40tr. Copetti/Photofab MCP/Rex Features 48bl. David
Fisher/Rex Features 14 (& 41br), 27tl, 57ml. David Lee/Shutterstock.com 43m. Debby Wong/Shutterstock.
com 40bl (hair). Dmitry Lobanov/Shutterstock.com 53tl. Dooley Productions/Shutterstock.com 29tl. EdwinAC/
Shutterstock.com 37b-4. Elizabeth Wu/Shutterstock.com 36b-3. Eric Isselée/shutterstock.com 52br. Everett
Collection/Rex Features 29mr. Featureflash/Shutterstock.com 16b-1 (& 20b-4), 20b-1, 20b-3, 20m-2,
21b-2, 36b-5, 37b-2, 37b-3, 37b-5, 47tl, 54bl, 56mr, 58tl. FlashStudio/Shutterstock.com 54br. Geoff
Moore/Rex Features 48tl. Helga Esteb/Shutterstock.com 10l, 16b-4, 19l, 20b-2, 20m-3, 21b-4, 40tl, 46bl,
51ml, 52ml, 56br. HitToon.com/Shutterstock.com 13br. ITV/Rex Features 2 (& 15, 40bl & 62), 8, 28ml, 47b,
50b. Ivan Bondarenko/Shutterstock.com 53bl. James Curley/Rex Features 16b-2 (& 20m-1). Jasenka Luka/
Shutterstock.com 50tr. Joe Seer/Shutterstock.com 18l, 53br, 58bl. Jonathan Hordle/Rex Features 19r, 57br.
Josemaria Toscano/Shutterstock.com 13bl. Ken McKay/Rex Features 17b, 17t, 21tr, 44, 47tr, 49t, 59br.
KeystoneUSA-ZUMA/Rex Features 30. Lehtikuva OY/Rex Features 31br. Lev Radin/Shutterstock.com 45mr. Lili
Forberg/Rex Features 26. Locote/Shutterstock.com 43bm. Losevsky Pavel/Shutterstock.com 13ml. Loskutnikov/
Shutterstock.com 42bl. Mark Salmon/Music Pics/Rex Features 21m. Mark St George/Rex Features 35, 37b-
1. Mastering_Microstock/Shutterstock.com 13tl. Nikshor/Shutterstock.com 51br. Nils Jorgensen/Rex Features
27tr, 32, 48br, 61br (& poster). Photosani/Shutterstock.com 42bm. Picture Perfect/Rex Features 10 (41bl &
back cover). Piers Alladyce/Rex Features 45tl. Rangizzz/Shutterstock.com 51mr. Ray Tang/Rex Features 56bl.
Rena Schild/Shutterstock.com 45ml. Rex Features 5 (& 36b-1 & front cover), 11r, 12, 16mr (& 55), 23, 24
(& 25 & 60), 33, 34m, 34ml, 34mr, 36b-2, 36b-4, 38b, 38m, 39, 45br, 46tr, 49bl, 49ml. Richard Young/
Rex Features 21b-1, 29bl. Robbi/Shutterstock.com 42br. Roman Sigaev/Shutterstock.com 42m, 43mr, 43tr.
Rook76/Shutterstock.com 52mr. Sari Gustafsson/Rex Features 22. Solent News & Photo Agency/Rex Features
59t. Steve Meddle/Rex Features 21mr. TSpider/shutterstock.com 42tr. Viktoriya/Shutterstock.com 43tl. Vince
Clements/Shutterstock.com 51tr. Vipflash/Shutterstock.com 28br. Vipflash/Shutterstock.com 41tl. Xavier Chi/
Shutterstock.com 12bg.

The Random House Group Limited supports The Forest Stewardship Council (FSC®), the leading international forest
certification organisation. Our books carrying the FSC label are printed on FSC® certified paper. FSC is the only
forest certification scheme endorsed by the leading environmental organisations, including Greenpeace. Our paper
procurement policy can be found at www.randomhouse.co.uk/environment

Bantam Books are published by
Random House Children's Books,
61–63 Uxbridge Road, London W5 5SA

www.**totallyrandombooks**.co.uk
www.**kidsatrandomhouse**.co.uk

Addresses for companies within The Random House Group Limited can be found at:
www.randomhouse.co.uk/offices.htm

THE RANDOM HOUSE GROUP Limited Reg. No. 954009

A CIP catalogue record for this book is available from the British Library.

Printed in Italy

100% UNOFFICIAL
JEDWARD

CONTENTS

THE GRIMES!

DID YOU KNOW?
John is always on the left, and Edward is on the right.

JEDWARD'S EARLY YEARS

Our favourite identical twins were born on 16th October 1991 at the Rotunda Hospital in Dublin, Ireland. Their parents called them **John Paul Henry Daniel Richard Grimes** and **Edward Peter Anthony Kevin Patrick Grimes** – what fantastic full names! John is ten minutes older than Edward.

The twins' father, John Senior, is a computer technician and their mother, Susannah, is a teacher. They have one older brother, who is called Kevin and is a law student.

John and Edward attended the Scoil Bhríde National School together, before moving first to the King's Hospital School and then to the Institute of Education.

The boys have always loved performing, particularly pop music, and they took part in many talent shows when they were at school. They say they are inspired by artists like Justin Timberlake, Britney Spears and the boy bands Backstreet Boys and *NSYNC. Totally pop-tastic!

DID YOU KNOW?
John's dream date would be Britney Spears, while Edward's would be Taylor Swift.

TWIN TRIVIA

Here are some fun Jedward facts and stats!

DATE OF BIRTH: 16th October 1991
FULL NAMES: John Paul Henry Daniel Richard Grimes and Edward Peter Anthony Kevin Patrick Grimes
PLACE OF BIRTH: Dublin, Ireland
PARENTS: Dad, John Senior and mum, Susannah
SIBLING: Brother, Kevin
HEIGHT: John is 5' 11" and Edward is 5' 10"
EYE COLOUR: Blue
HAIR COLOUR: Blond
STAR SIGN: Libra
X FACTOR MENTOR: Louis Walsh
RECORD LABEL: Universal

DID YOU KNOW?

The twins are talented athletes and are members of Dundrum South Dublin Athletic Club. They once came 7th and 13th in an Irish schools' mountain running championship!

ALL ABOUT

How much do you know about John and Edward's home country? Find out by answering these quick questions!

Draw it here!

1. The Irish flag is made up of which three colours?
2. How many leaves does a shamrock have?
3. Ireland's national day is called what?
4. What is the capital city of the Republic of Ireland?
5. What is the capital city of Northern Ireland?
6. A short, funny poem is called what?
7. Who is *The X Factor*'s Irish judge?
8. What is Ireland's colourful nickname?
9. The Republic of Ireland uses which currency?
10. Ireland and the UK are separated by which sea?

RRRAAAARRRRR!!

Croke Park, Dublin

IRELAND

River Liffey, Dublin

City Hall, Belfast

DID YOU KNOW?

On 23rd May 2011, Jedward performed in front of 60,000 people at College Green in Dublin, ahead of a speech by visiting U.S. President, Barack Obama.

13

JED-WORDSEARCH

There are many wonderful, wacky words that describe the twins! Can you find the fifteen words below in the giant grid?

Colourful

Loud

Singers

Energetic

Irish

Happy

Twins

Unique

Celebrities

Enthusiastic

Lively

Performers

Fun

Bonkers

Dancers

```
P S T V L I V E L Y X C
B E S L O U D C F P R E
K C R U K F D E G P O L
G I E F U N Q N J A D E
X R G R O V U E B H B B
L I N U H R J R O I O R
U S I O R C M G V O N I
N H S L I O L E D J K T
I D C O G B X T R K E I
Q P U C R T W I N S R E
U P W F D A N C E R S S
E N T H U S I A S T I C
```

TWINS WITH THE X FACTOR!

It was after auditioning for The X Factor that John and Edward became Jedward! Let's learn more about their time on the top TV talent show . . .

In 2009, *The X Factor* was on its 6th series and was still one of the most popular programmes on TV. The judges were Louis Walsh, Dannii Minogue, Cheryl Cole and, of course, Simon Cowell, and when they landed in Glasgow for the next round of auditions, they were in for a surprise!

The twins, then performing as 'John & Edward', burst onto the stage and began to sing 'As Long As You Love Me' by the Backstreet Boys. SiCo said 'no', cutting them off after just one verse and telling them they had American accents, but Dannii and Louis both said 'yes'. Cheryl, who had the deciding vote, sent them through to the Bootcamp stage.

Jedward then made it to the Judges' Houses section of the show, with fellow Irishman Louis as their mentor in the Groups category. He saw something special in the boisterous boys and picked them as one of his acts to perform on the Live Shows!

Their cheeky song choices included 'Rock DJ' by Robbie Williams, 'She Bangs' by Ricky Martin and a mash-up of Queen's 'Under Pressure' and Vanilla Ice's 'Ice Ice Baby'. They even sang the theme tune from the 'Ghostbusters' movie and wore boiler suits, with backing-dancers dressed as ghosts!

Their enthusiastic, entertaining and memorable performances won them many votes and meant they survived to week seven. They finished in 6th place when the judges chose to save Olly Murs in an amazing sing-off, and the show was eventually won by Joe McElderry.

But it wasn't the end of the road for our favourite twins! They went on to be managed by their *X Factor* mentor Louis and have since released several records. Go Jedward!

The boys get styled up on 24th October 2009.

'Look at Madonna: she isn't the best singer but, like the twins, she is a great entertainer.'

Louis Walsh, Jedward's manager

John and Edward talk to Holly Willoughby and Phillip Schofield on *This Morning* after leaving *The X Factor*.

THE JUDGES ON

Jedward definitely divided the judges when they appeared on The X Factor! Here we reveal what they said about the twins . . .

Surly Simon

Simon Cowell, known for his brutal honesty and witty put-downs, stopped the twins mid-audition and called them 'vile', which was a little mean! After one of their songs, he said that if someone heard it on the radio, it would probably be one of the worst things they'd ever heard. And apparently that was Simon attempting to be constructive! They proved to be popular with the viewers though and as time went on, even SiCo began to warm to them a little, telling the twins, 'I have to judge you in Jedward land and if I'm there, that has to be your best performance. There's no point getting angry, if people like you, they like you.' Eventually he even admitted that he was actually going to miss them. Good work, Jedward!

Disapproving Dannii

Dannii Minogue was never a huge Jedward fan, stating on several occasions that the twins couldn't sing and so it was unfair on the other, more 'vocally talented' contestants. She said she wished all the good *singers* luck in the *singing* competition! Dannii did enjoy some of their entertaining on-stage displays though, telling them that she was torn and although their singing was not the same standard as the previous winner, Alexandra Burke, it was still a great performance. Sadly, it wasn't enough to win her vote and she ended their time on *The X Factor*, stating, 'I'm going to have to judge it as I've judged it the whole time. On the premise that it's a singing competition I will have to send home John and Edward.' Bad luck, boys!

JEDWARD

'If you only get good comments, it doesn't make you work harder. If they say negative things, it only makes us get more determined.'

Edward, one half of Jedward

Cheerful Cheryl

Cheryl Cole loved the cheeky chaps from the second they first stepped onto the *X Factor* stage and it was her vote that sent them through to Bootcamp. They were pretty pleased when she told them after one performance that they were her 'guilty pleasure' and the ones she really looked forward to watching. She was sad when the time came for her to vote them out of the competition, saying, 'Boys, I've really loved you over the past few weeks and big kisses... but the act I'm going to send home is John and Edward.' Cheryl described the twins as two of the nicest kids she'd ever met, something which is bound to have brought a smile to the boys' faces!

Lively Louis

Louis Walsh was Jedward's strongest supporter from the start, and luckily for them he was chosen to mentor the Groups category. He saw their huge potential, passionately declaring that he thought the twins could win it because they might not be the best singers or dancers, but they're brilliant entertainers. When their luck on the show finally ran out, Louis told Jedward he'd had the best time working with them and that they'd made him feel young again. And he knew they weren't finished yet! Their mentor soon became their manager and he lined up lots of things to keep the boys busy . . . 'They're probably going to do a TV series, endorsements, gigging, a bit of singing, a bit of dancing. Kids love them. I can see Jedward dolls, Jedward books, Jedward everything, Jedward mania.' We're so happy to hear we'll be seeing lots more of Jedward!

JUMBLED JUDGES

Unscramble the letters to reveal all the X Factor judges, past and present, and then match the names to the pictures!

1 ONSMI =
2 CRYHLE =
3 NIADNI =
4 SOILU =
5 TASULI =
6 RYAG =
7 LKYEL =

A

B

C

D

E

F

G

20

AND THE WINNER IS

Can you remember all the X Factor's victorious acts? Try to match the winners to the year that they won!

Alexandra Burke
Leona Lewis
Steve Brookstein
Leon Jackson
Little Mix
Matt Cardle
Shayne Ward
Joe McElderry

2004
2005
2010
2007
2011
2009
2008
2006

JEDWARD CROSSWORD

Use the clues to complete this Jedward crossword!

Across:

1 Jedward's *Eurovision* song.
3 The twins' brother.
6 Jedward's record company.
8 Jedward's star sign.
9 John and Edward's last name.
11 The boys' birth month.
12 Jedward's place in *Celebrity Big Brother*.
14 Jedward's *X Factor* mentor.
15 The winner of the 6th series of *The X Factor*.

Down:

2 Jedward's home country.
4 Jedward's most famous feature.
5 The city where Jedward auditioned for *The X Factor*.
7 Jedward represented Ireland in this song contest.
10 The talent show that made Jedward famous.
13 The band that represented the UK in *Eurovision*.

There are ten differences between these two pictures of the twins. Can you circle them all?

SEEING

DOUBLE DOUBLE

SINGING STARS

Record label Sony Music snapped up Jedward straight away and the song chosen for the twins' debut single was one they'd performed on *The X Factor*, 'Under Pressure (Ice Ice Baby)'. Vanilla Ice, aka Robert Matthew Van Winkle, even appeared on the track and performed with them at the National Television Awards in 2010! It was a number 1 hit in the Irish singles chart and a number 2 hit in the UK singles chart on downloads alone – not at all bad for a first attempt!

Jedward then moved labels, from Sony to Universal. There they signed a three-album deal and released their second single, a cover of Blink-182's 'All the Small Things'. Since then, the twins have released two awesome albums which have gone down a storm all around Europe, and have been particularly popular in their home country of Ireland.

Their first album, entitled 'Planet Jedward', consisted entirely of cover songs and was released in July 2010. It became the fastest selling record in Ireland that year, reaching number 1 in the Irish albums chart, and it also climbed to number 17 on the UK albums chart. When they went on the Planet Jedward tour, new dates had to be added due to high demand!

Only original songs featured on album number two, which was called 'Victory' and was released in August 2011. The first single from it, 'Lipstick', reached number 1 in the Irish charts, as did their second single, 'Bad Behaviour'. The boys were on a roll and riding high in the charts!

We can't wait to hear what their third album will be like . . .

After their exit from The X Factor, Jedward kept on singing. Here's more on their fun-tastic musical career so far . . .

With Vanilla Ice at the National Television Awards in 2010.

Promoting their first album.

NAME THAT SONG

See if you can name the songs that Jedward performed on The X Factor, plus the original artists!

1

- Jedward sang this song for their *X Factor* audition.
- Simon Cowell cut them off after just one verse.
- The song is by a popular US boy band, originally with five members.
- It was a single from the band's debut album.

Song title:

Artist:

2

- This was one of the songs Jedward performed at the Judges' Houses stage.
- They performed in front of mentor Louis Walsh and guest judge Ronan Keating.
- The song is by a band with three members, including twin brothers, and it was their second single.

Song title:

Artist:

3

- Jedward sang this song in week 1 of the live shows, and again as their week 5 survival song.
- The song is by a solo artist who was once a member of a popular boy band.
- It was on his fourth solo album and had a controversial music video.
- The first time they performed the song, Jedward were lowered onto the stage and wore black and white suits.

Song title:

Artist:

- Jedward sang this song in week 2 of the live shows.
- The song is by a female solo singer and was the title track on her second album.
- She is also a former *Disney's The Mickey Mouse Club* star.
- Jedward wore shiny red suits for the performance.

Song title:

Artist:

- Jedward sang this song in week 5 of the live shows.
- The song is taken from a 1980's film, which has the same name.
- **The film starred actors Bill Murray and Dan Aykroyd.**
- Jedward wore iconic outfits and flew onto the stage.

Song title:

Artist:

- Jedward sang this mash-up of two songs in week 6 of the live shows.
- The songs are by a British rock band with four members, and an American rapper.
- Jedward wore shiny silver suits when they sang this song.
- They later released a cover of one of the songs as their first single.

Song titles:

Artists:

'I love watching them. If someone said to me I had to go and watch a gig of the X Factor contestants . . . who do [I] want to see? I'd love to go and watch Jedward!'

Robbie Williams, pop star

ENTERTAINING

Jedward took Europe by storm in 2011, with a performance to remember in the Eurovision Song Contest!

We were so happy when we heard that Jedward had been chosen to represent Ireland at *Eurovision* in 2011! They couldn't have picked more perfect performers for the colourful, cheesy song contest!

It was the 56th contest and was held in Düsseldorf, Germany, which was the previous year's winning country. The awesome Esprit Arena, the venue for the event, is a multifunctional football stadium that can seat 54,600 people and has a closable roof.

The twins' song was called 'Lipstick' and the boys bounced onto the stage wearing bright, big-shouldered sparkly jackets in lipstick-red. They put on a typically energetic and enthusiastic performance and made Ireland proud by coming in 8th place.

The UK's entry was newly-reformed boy band Blue, who wore the colour that matches their name. Their song was called 'I Can', but unfortunately they couldn't win the contest for their country and came in 11th place. Jedward beat Blue! Well done boys!

In the end, Eurovision 2011 was won by Azerbaijan's singers Eldar and Nigar with their romantic duet, 'Running Scared' . . .

There are rumours that the twins are set to perform for Ireland in the contest again next year, so watch this space and keep your fingers crossed!

The winners Eldar and Nigar from Azerbaijan.

EUROPE!

'Eurovision has transformed us into superheroes with our own special powers! Our No. 1 power is having the best fans!'

Edward, one half of Jedward

Sorry, Blue — Jedward beat you!

In this battle of the boy bands, answer the questions to find out which pop group you prefer!

BAM

1 Do you prefer records that are:
a Powerful pop songs?
b Mad musical mash-ups?

2 Do you like dance moves to be:
a Perfect and precise?
b Big and bold?

3 Do you like boy bands to wear:
a Only the coolest clothes?
b Always outrageous outfits?

4 Do you love hair that's in:
a A sleek style?
b A sky-high style?

THE BOYS

SOK

VS BLUE

5 Do you like boy bands where the members are:
- **a** Friends?
- **b** Family?

6 What style do you like a boy band to have:
- **a** Subtle and stylish?
- **b** Loud and proud?

7 Do you love boy bands that were popular:
- **a** In the past?
- **b** In the present?

Mostly A's.
You like Blue!
They really can sing, and have some amazing dance moves, too. They are truly professional performers!

Mostly B's.
You like the boys!
They love to have fun and don't take life, or singing, too seriously. They are totally energetic entertainers!

THE BOYS AND

The troublesome twosome causing chaos in the *Celebrity Big Brother* house? That was something we couldn't wait to see! And the boisterous boys didn't disappoint, making a mess and playing pranks at every opportunity. Their fellow 'celebs', including the bubbly beautician Amy Childs, awesome actor Lucien Laviscount and amazing model Bobby Sabel, didn't know what had hit them when the Jedward whirlwind blew into the house!

By 2011, Jedward were so famous that they were wanted for Celebrity Big Brother. Awesome!

Jedward's highlights in the house included going on a supermarket sweep, where they bought SO many sweets, and winning a contest to see who could hold a cheesy smile for the longest. The twins were also separated for one task, which was a sad time for both of the boys and for us!

In the end, they came in 3rd place, with Kerry Katona as the runner up and Paddy Doherty being crowned the winner. They certainly weren't losers though, as their appearance is said to have added £1 million to their £3.5 million fortune!

Despite all the drama they caused, the twins didn't receive a single nomination during their time in the house. The other celebs must have loved Jedward as much as we do! And after leaving the CBB house, Jedward said, 'We had an awesome time, was so cool being in there. They all rocked!'

BIG BROTHER!

KABOOM!

35

CBB FACT FILE!

Let's take a closer look at the 2011 Celebrity Big Brother contestants . . .

	Jedward	Bobby Sabel	Pamela Bach-Hasselhoff	Lucien Laviscount	Sally Bercow
Birthday	16th October 1991	5th August 1986	16th October 1963	9th June 1992	22nd November 1969
Home town	Dublin	London	Tulsa in Oklahoma, America	Ribble Valley, Lancashire	London
Famous for	Pop stars	International model	Actress and producer	Actor	Wife of the Speaker of the House of Commons
Fun fact	They tried to say 'OK' 100 times during an interview on OK! TV.	He has graced catwalks in the fashion capitals of the world, including Milan, New York and Paris.	Pamela is an accredited lifeguard and certified scuba diver.	He has modelled for David Beckham's clothing range.	She did a newspaper interview dressed in a bed sheet.
CBB place	3rd	7th	9th	5th	10th

	Darryn Lyons	Amy Childs	Paddy Doherty	Tara Reid	Kerry Katona
Birthday	19th August 1965	14th June 1990	6th February 1959	8th November 1975	6th September 1980
Home town	Geelong in Victoria, Australia	Brentwood, Essex	Wherever his family are	Wyckoff, New Jersey	Warrington
Famous for	Member of the Paparazzi	Beautician and TV personality (*The Only Way Is Essex* and *It's All About Amy*)	TV personality (*Big Fat Gypsy Weddings*)	Actress	Television presenter, actress and singer
Fun fact	Darryn loves interior design.	Amy was once a member of the Essex County Table Tennis team.	He has 5 children and 15 grandchildren.	Tara once booked a London hotel room just for her shoes!	Kerry was once in girl band Atomic Kitten.
CBB place	6th	4th	1st - the winner!	8th	2nd

THE JED HEAD

The twins have become known for their trademark hair – huge, high, gravity-defying quiffs. It's even rumoured that they had an extra clause written into their *Celebrity Big Brother* contract, to make sure they didn't have to take part in any task that involved cutting their hair. Now, that's some special hair! And here's how you can get quiff-tastic too, in three simple steps . . .

Jed Head Essentials:
- Top-heavy hair
- Masses of mousse
- Huge amounts of hairspray
- A super-powerful hairdryer

Step 1
First, make sure your hair is clean, then add masses of mousse while it's still wet.

Step 2
Next, hang your head upside-down and blast your hair with the dryer.

Step 3
Finally, when your hair is dry and standing up stiffly, start hairspraying!

DID YOU KNOW?
Jedward have revealed that their hair has been insured for £1 million!

If your hair isn't suitable to style into a quiff, here's another way to get the Jedward look. Just cut out and add elastic!

CUT OUT QUIFF

MIXED-UP MANES

Ever wondered what Jedward would look like with a new 'do? And should other celebs start sporting a quiff? Let's take a look . . .

JUSTIN BIEBER

The popular young popstar has probably the most famous hair in the world right now! Does he look as cute with a quiff?

CHERYL COLE

The super-glamorous Girls Aloud star has a gorgeous, glossy mane. Would the twins suit long locks like hers?

LADY GAGA

Lady Gaga is a colourful character who loves to wear wild and wacky wigs! For her next look, should she try a quiff?

HARRY STYLES

Perhaps the most popular member of boy band One Direction, handsome Harry has curly hair. Would Jedward suit his style?

ALL ABOUT TWO

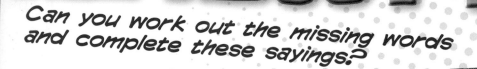

Can you work out the missing words and complete these sayings?

1. Two wrongs don't make a _ _ _ _ _.

2. Two _ _ _ _ _ are better than one.

3. Two's company, _ _ _ _ _'s a crowd.

4. There are two _ _ _ _ _ to every story.

5. One for the money, two for the _ _ _ _.

6. A _ _ _ _ in the hand is worth two in the bush.

7. Like two _ _ _ _ in a pod.

8. _ _ _ _ _ on your own two feet.

9 No two _ _ _ _ about it.

10 A _ _ _ _ of two halves.

11 Kill two birds with one _ _ _ _ _.

12 One step _ _ _ _ _ _ _ and two steps back.

13 One, two, _ _ _ _ _ _ my shoe.

14 Two _ _ _ _ _ _ that beat as one.

JEDWARD JIGSAW

Match the pieces to the spaces to complete this Jedward jigsaw! Which piece is not part of the puzzle?

OTHER CELEB TWINS

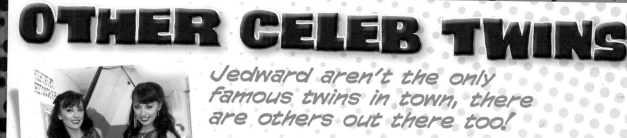

Jedward aren't the only famous twins in town, there are others out there too!

The Cheeky Girls

Monica and Gabriela Irimia, who are originally from Transylvania, auditioned for *Popstars: The Rivals* in 2002. The judges were lost for words and the girls didn't make it through. They did have some success though, later releasing 'Cheeky Song' and 'Take Your Shoes Off', which both did surprisingly well in the charts.

Mary-Kate and Ashley Olsen

These gorgeous girls starred in the US sitcom *Full House* when they were really young, and went on to star in other TV shows and films. Later they launched their own fashion and make-up lines and became known as style icons. They are worth an estimated $100 million!

Scarlett and Hunter Johansson

Stunning Scarlett is a super-successful film star, known around the world. But did you know she had a twin brother? His name is Hunter, and he didn't follow his sister to Hollywood. Instead the path he chose was politics, with a career as a campaign organiser for Barack Obama.

Knox Léon and Vivienne Marcheline Jolie-Pitt

Brad Pitt and Angelina Jolie's twins were born in Nice, France, on 12th July 2008. Brad and Angelina sold exclusive photos of their babies to *People* magazine and *Hello!* magazine for $14 million, and gave the money to charity. Those photos are rumoured to be the most expensive celebrity pictures ever taken!

THE TWINS ON TV

As well as singing and dancing on stage, the twins have also appeared on TV several times . . .

As well as their time on *The X Factor* and in the *Celebrity Big Brother* house, the twins starred in their own reality TV show, called *OMG: It's Jedward!*. It was a one-hour documentary for Irish television, and showed them promoting their first album, 'Planet Jedward', with endless signings and energetic performances.

Then came a 3-part series, *Jedward: Let Loose*, which followed the boys moving out of their family home and into a brand new apartment of their own in Dublin. Watching them learn to cook, clean and fend for themselves for the first time made for some very entertaining viewing!

With Darryn Lyons and Kerry Katona after *CBB*.

The twins also appeared in *Jedward's Big Adventure*, where they attempted to guide real tourists around Britain. They were given five world heritage sites, told to learn some fascinating facts, and then paired with some celeb guests, including *Big Brother* presenter Brian Dowling and girl band Parade. It was an awesome adventure indeed!

And after their dream of fame and fortune had come true, the boys wanted to make the dreams of some of their fans come true, too! In the 10-part series, *OMG! Jedward's Dream Factory*, the twins helped many 8 to 16 year olds to train with their favourite football team or go shopping with a soap star.

DID YOU KNOW?
Jedward were signed to Next Models and appeared in fashion magazines such as *i-D, Esquire* and *Grazia*.

Performing 'Wow Oh Wow' on *This Morning*.

Performing 'Wow Oh Wow' on *This Morning*.

Jedward have also appeared regularly on the comedy panel show, *Celebrity Juice*. Each week they compete against the show's host, Keith Lemon, in various tasks. Lemon even makes sure he looks like the twins, by styling his hair in a quiff – hilarious!

We're sure there will be even more TV shows for Jedward fans in the near future! We can't wait to see what the twins have in the pipeline . . .

In their new flat on *Jedward: Let Loose*.

PHOTO FUN!

The twins are known for their crazy quotes! What do you think they're saying here? Fill in the blank speech bubbles with some wacky Jed-words . . .

BLAF!

WHICH TWIN . . .

How well do you know the dynamic duo? Put your twin knowledge to the test with this quick-fire quiz!

1 Which twin . . . hurt his knee when performing at T4 On The Beach?

John ☐   Edward ☐

2 Which twin . . . would like to date talented singer Taylor Swift?

John ☐   Edward ☐

3 Which twin . . . won bronze in a 1,500m race?

John ☐
Edward ☐

4 Which twin . . . has a pointy right ear?

John ☐   Edward ☐

5 Which twin . . . always stands on the right?

John ☐   Edward ☐

6 Which twin . . . is ten minutes older?

John ☐

Edward ☐

7 Which twin . . . is a little bit taller?

John ☐   Edward ☐

8 Which twin . . . is the messiest?

John ☐   Edward ☐

JEDWARD'S FAVOURITES

Here are a few of Jedward's favourite things!

Food: Sushi

Animal: Dogs

Female celebs: Taylor Swift (Edward) and Britney Spears (John)

Sport: Running

Item of clothing: Skinny jeans

TV shows: *Friends* (and Chandler is their favourite character!) and *The Simpsons*

Films: *Toy Story*, *Home Alone* and *Titanic*

X Factor judges: Simon Cowell and Louis Walsh

Words: Cool, crazy and awesome

Superhero: Superman

JEDWARD'S FIRSTS AND LASTS

Now let's look at some of the twins' firsts and lasts . . .

First thing they think of when they wake up: Their fans.

Last time they were star struck: When they met Paul McCartney.

First thing they would do if they ran the country: Have a John and Edward Appreciation Day.

Last big purchase they made: Laptop computers.

First great advice they were ever given: Just be yourself and be grateful for everything you have.

First record they ever bought was by: *NSYNC

Last lie they told: A small, jokey white lie. Lying is bad!

First time they realised they were famous: When they heard themselves on the radio.

Last meal on earth would be: Sushi.

THE GRIMES DO GOOD

When Jedward were asked to star in an anti-bullying campaign for The Irish Society for the Prevention of Cruelty to Children (The ISPCC), along with their *X Factor* mentor, Louis Walsh, they jumped at the chance.

The twins featured in a celebrity-fronted campaign in Ireland, which aimed to stop bullying in schools and communities. It was started by fellow singer and ISPCC ambassador, Mark Feehily, from the world-famous boy band, Westlife.

When talking about why they wanted to get involved in the campaign, John and Edward said, 'We were bullied at school but we were lucky in one way as we had each other. We know firsthand how horrible bullying can be and so we jumped at the opportunity of being part of this campaign.'

The adverts are hard-hitting and show the usually happy-go-lucky lads in a very different light. They want to help others who are going through what they themselves experienced at school, and we think that's truly wonderful. It makes us love the twins even more than before!

The boys wanted to use their new-found fame to do some good, so they joined a campaign that's close to their hearts . . .

Louis Walsh and Westlife: Kian Egan, Mark Feehily, Shane Filan and Nicky Byrne

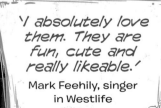

'I absolutely love them. They are fun, cute and really likeable.'

Mark Feehily, singer in Westlife

MEMORABLE MOMENTS

Jedward have given us many memorable moments over the years! We think these are their top ten . . .

1 While the twins were singing 'Under Pressure/Ice Ice Baby' live on *The X Factor*, DJ Calvin Harris stormed the stage, holding a pineapple on his head. The twins carried on singing and dancing, proving they are true professionals!

2 We'll never forget the twins' mesmerizing 'Ghostbusters' performance on *The X Factor* – they really went all-out and even Simon Cowell had to smile!

3 When Jedward were interviewed on *Friday Night With Jonathon Ross*, they totally stole the show. The twins talked non-stop and Wossy struggled to get a word in edgeways!

4 Jedward's enthusiastic *Eurovision* performance won them even more fans across Europe and made Ireland proud! And we want their super-sparkly jackets!

5 In that awesome advert for Dragon Quest IX on the Nintendo DS, the twins talk about dressing up the characters before going into battle – with bunny ears! In Jedward's own words, 'Ooh la la!'

6 As the boys bounced around on stage on eviction night, wearing bright blue blazers with gold sparkly arm bands, anyone would have thought they'd won *Celebrity Big Brother* instead of coming 3rd!

7 It was a dream come true for the twins when they performed with their idol, pop princess Britney Spears, at the O2 arena on 28th October 2011. They described it as 'the coolest thing eveeeeeeer!'

8 At the National Television Awards in 2010, Jedward performed 'Under Pressure (Ice Ice Baby)' with Vanilla Ice. It's not often you see three total legends on stage together!

9 During a performance of 'Ghostbusters' at T4 On The Beach, Edward hurt his knee when he landed badly after a jump. But he carried on to the end of the song, by hopping on one leg. That twin is such a trooper!

10 When the boys got to leave the *CBB* house to go on a shopping spree, they filled the trolley with a few bits of food, but mostly with candy. The other housemates weren't impressed with their sweet-tooth choices!

A-Z OF JEDWARD

This is your ULTIMATE guide to the Grimes twins!

A Accent The boys have lovely Irish accents.

B Britney Spears Their idol!

C Celebrity Big Brother The twins came 3rd.

D Dublin The Irish city where the boys were born.

E Edward One half of Jedward.

F Fans They are so important to the twins!

G Grimes John and Edward's last name.

H Happy-go-lucky lads The boys have fun wherever they go!

I International stars Against all odds, the boys have won fans from around the world!

J John The other half of Jedward.

K Kevin The boys' older brother.

L Lipstick Jedward's *Eurovision* song, representing Ireland.

M Mentor and manager Louis Walsh took both of these roles.

N Nintendo DS The twins starred in adverts for the Dragon Quest IX game.

O October The boys' birthday month.

P Planet Jedward The title of their first album.

Q Quiffs Jedward's signature 'do!

R Running The twins' top sport.

S Sushi Their favourite food.

T **Taylor Swift** She's the singer Edward would like to date.

U **Universal** The record label representing Jedward.

V **Victory** Their second album.

W **Wacky wardrobe** The twins are known for their crazy, colourful clothes.

X **X Factor** The show that shot John and Edward Grimes to fame!

Y **Yeah!** This is one of Jedward's most-used words.

Z **Zzzz** The boys have boundless energy and just watching them makes us feel tired!

So, who's your top twin, John or Edward? We think the boys are BOTH brilliant!

ALL THE ANSWERS

Page 12 All About Ireland

1) Green, white and orange
2) Three
3) St. Patrick's Day
4) Dublin
5) Belfast
6) A limerick
7) Louis Walsh
8) The Emerald Isle
9) The Euro
10) The Irish Sea

Page 14 Jed-wordsearch

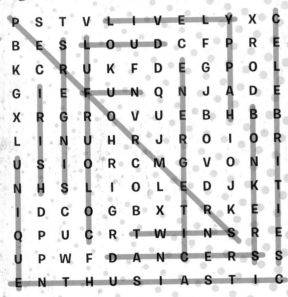

Page 20 Jumbled Judges

1) C, Simon
2) E, Cheryl
3) A, Dannii
4) G, Louis
5) F, Tulisa
6) B, Gary
7) D, Kelly

Page 21 And The Winner Is . . .

Steve Brookstein – 2004
Shayne Ward – 2005
Leona Lewis – 2006
Leon Jackson – 2007
Alexandra Burke – 2008
Joe McElderry – 2009
Matt Cardle – 2010
Little Mix – 2011

Page 22 Jedward Crossword

See above right

Page 24 Seeing Double

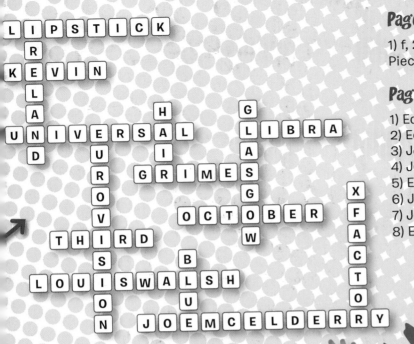

LIPSTICK
IRELAND
KEVIN
UNIVERSAL
EUROVISION
GLASGOW
HILARY GRIMES
LIBRA
OCTOBER
XFACTOR
THIRD
LOUISWALSH
JOEMCELDERRY

Page 44 Jedward Jigsaw

1) f, 2) b, 3) c, 4) e, 5) a.
Piece d is not part of the puzzle.

Page 50 Which Twin . . .

1) Edward
2) Edward
3) John
4) John
5) Edward
6) John
7) John
8) Edward

Page 28 Name That Song

1) 'As Long As You Love Me' by The Backstreet Boys
2) 'When Will I Be Famous?' by Bros
3) 'Rock DJ' by Robbie Williams
4) 'Oops!... I Did It Again' by Britney Spears
5) 'Ghostbusters' by Ray Parker, Jr.
6) 'Under Pressure' by Queen, with 'Ice Ice Baby' by Vanilla Ice

Page 42 All About Two

1) right
2) heads
3) three
4) sides
5) show
6) bird
7) peas
8) stand
9) ways
10) game
11) stone
12) forward
13) buckle
14) hearts